The Chrysler Building: The History of One of New York City's Most Famous Landmarks

By Charles River Editors

The Chrysler Building in 1932

About Charles River Editors

Charles River Editors provides superior editing and original writing services across the digital publishing industry, with the expertise to create digital content for publishers across a vast range of subject matter. In addition to providing original digital content for third party publishers, we also republish civilization's greatest literary works, bringing them to new generations of readers via ebooks.

Introduction

David Shankbone's picture of the Chrysler Building

The Chrysler Building

"I would give the greatest sunset in the world for one sight of New York's skyline. The shapes and the thought that made them. The sky over New York and the will of man made visible... Let them come to New York, stand on the shore of the Hudson, look and kneel. When I see the city from my window - no, I don't feel how small I am - but I feel that if a war came to threaten this, I would like to throw myself into space, over the city, and protect these buildings with my body." – Ayn Rand, *The Fountainhead*

Of all the great cities in the world, few personify their country like New York City. As America's largest city and best known immigration gateway into the country, the Big Apple represents the beauty, diversity and sheer strength of the United States, a global financial center that has enticed people chasing the "American Dream" for centuries.

Given that history, it's no surprise that New Yorkers have always wanted to construct the biggest and best structures possible, even in the early 1930s at the height of the Great Depression. Indeed, those years produced the Empire State Building, which remains the city's most iconic building, but New York's most famous skyscraper wouldn't have been possible without the Chrysler Building, a landmark in its own right that was the tallest building in the world for nearly a year before its more famous counterpart's completion. In fact, the spirit of competition between the groups working on the two buildings helped ensure that both look like they do today, and the Chrysler Building only reached the height it did because a large skyscraper at 40 Wall Street was also trying to claim the mantle of tallest building at the same time.

The Chrysler Building was the first manmade object to surpass 1,000 feet in height, and while it has been surpassed by considerably taller projects since, it remains the largest steel-supported brick building in the world. As its name suggests, the Chrysler Building was named after Walter P. Chrysler, who ran the car company at the time, and yet his corporation never owned the building because he cherished it so much that he personally paid for the skyscraper and kept it in his family. Although it has since been sold to new groups, the name has remained, and the Chrysler Building continues to be a conspicuous part of the skyline in Midtown.

The Chrysler Building: The History of New York City's Most Iconic Landmark chronicles the construction and history of the one of the Big Apple's most famous buildings. Along with pictures of important people, places, and events, you will learn about the Chrysler Building like never before, in no time at all.

The Chrysler Building: The History of One of New York City's Most Famous Landmarks

About Charles River Editors

Introduction

Chapter 1: A Choice Piece of Land

A picture of the early stages of construction on the Chrysler Building

"The Chrysler Building would not look as it does if Dreamland had not burned down in 1911. Coney Island's white-towered Freudian fairway had been the brainchild of a real estate entrepreneur named William H. Reynolds, whose reputation for public mayhem was such that when a short circuit in the 'Hell Gate' exhibit set the entire blocks long place ablaze, some newspapers assumed that it was just another stunt. Financially drained and cured of his taste for artificial fantasy, Reynolds turned his attention to the real-life fantasy of Manhattan, where he proposed to erect the tallest building in the world. Although the Woolworth Building beat him to the punch, in 1913, and the war slowed him down, by the time the late-twenties boom began he had got hold of a choice piece of land at the new city hub around Grand Central Terminal, and had hired William Van Alen to execute the design. As the association suggests, Van Alen had a reputation of his own as a showman, albeit one in thrall to the most coolly modern materials and means." – Claudia Roth Pierpoint, "The Silver Spire" (*New Yorker* November 18, 2002)

The Woolworth Building

The story of the Chrysler Building is in many ways the story of one's man's determination to build the tallest building in the world, but it does not start out, as one might expect, with Walter Chrysler. Instead, the story begins with William Reynolds, a man who never built a car in his life. More than anything, Reynolds was a realtor and a master of self-promotion; prior to his involvement with what became the Chrysler Building, he was best known for Dreamland Park, located on New York's famed Coney Island. However, when his beautiful park burned to the ground in 1911, he turned his attention elsewhere, always looking for something new he could throw himself into.

Chrysler

SENATOR Wm. H. REYNOLDS, President. DREAMLAND

Reynolds

Reynolds' Dreamland on Coney Island

Eventually, Reynolds leased a large piece of land at the corner of Lexington Avenue and 42nd Street with the understanding that he would develop a significant structure on the property, but after years of procrastination, Reynolds finally hired architect William Van Alen in 1927 to draw up plans for a 40 story skyscraper for the site. Van Alen was respected in the business for his work on the Ablemarle office building in New York in partnership with Craig Severance. A 1924 article in the *Architectural Review* praised Van Alen but ignored Severance in referring to it as "William Van Alen's work," and that helped break up the partnership. This was ultimately a good thing, as Severance was more traditional in his designs and Van Alen's style was distinctly modern. For his own part, Van Alen explained his philosophy: "In designing a skyscraper there is no precedent to follow for the reason that we are using a new structural material, steel, which has been developed in America and is different in every way from the masonry construction of the past. Structurally, and in their purpose, our tall buildings are wholly unlike any buildings of an earlier day. To apply to our tall office buildings, apartment houses and hotels the familiar architectural features characteristic of the comparatively low palaces, temples and churches that were built before the advent of steel as a building material, is not economical or practical, and it is artistically wrong since it is not truthful."

Van Alen

Van Alen had plenty of admirers. In fact, fellow architect Richard Haviland Smythe once observed, "Van Alen's stuff is so darned clever that I don't know whether to admire it or hate it." Chesley Bonestell worked with Van Alen and a number of other architects, and he would go on to assert, "To my mind, Van Alen was the best of the modern architects of the period, and the Chrysler Building expresses New York of the time better than any other building."

Once he began work for Reynolds, Van Alen found himself caught up in the spirit of competition pervading the 1920s. Like great adventurers daring each other to go higher, the men leading the projects to develop new skyscrapers constantly announced that their buildings would actually be the tallest in the city. According to one magazine of the day, "In a rich baritone voice,

Van Alen sang something to the effect that only a block away he proposed putting up a fifty-six-story building! This, of course, made the Lincoln [building] people perfectly furious so they proclaimed that they would probably make theirs sixty-three stories high, to which Mr. Van Alen said, 'Hold, men, we will make ours SIXTY-FIVE stories high!'"

In April 1928, Reynolds secured a 67 year lease on his property and put the final piece in place for his magnificent plan, which was to be a "successful addition to the skyscraper group of mid-Manhattan [that will] serve to revolutionize store values and the class of tenants in 42nd Street and Lexington Avenue." When Van Alen's completed drawings were released the following August, the *American Architect* praised him, saying he "has departed from certain of the old-time principles on which the skyscraper was developed . . . the design of the Reynolds Building is developed to be of interest throughout its entire height."

With the design now in place, Reynolds sold his lease, his plans, and even the services of his architect to Walter P. Chrysler, head of the great automotive family. The negotiations were complicated and drawn out, with Nicolas Kelley, Chrysler's chief negotiator, writing a day-by-day account that included the following:

October 5—"After a long harrowing day, we passed one stage"

October 9—"I went into a difficult meeting with lawyers who have been treating us as if we were rogues"

October 10—"The whirl still continues"

October 13—"Here it is five o'clock on the warmest, muggiest and most drizzling of Saturday afternoons. We are making progress with our land deal"

October 16—"We closed the Chrysler land business yesterday!"

Finally, the Associated Press was able to inform the public: "The project to erect one of the tallest buildings m the world on Lexington Avenue opposite the Grand Central station has been taken over by Walter P. Chrysler and the building will be called the Chrysler building, it was announced today. The W. P. Chrysler Building Corp. has acquired the 66-year lease on the property which extends from 42nd to 43rd street, from Senator William H. Reynolds. Mr. Chrysler said the transaction was entirely personal and in no way connected with the Chrysler Motor Corp. Plans call for a 68-story building, 608 feet high, exceeding the height of the Woolworth building by 16 -feet. The project, appraised at $14,000,000, will be financed by S. W. Straus."

Once he was told that his project was in the hands of someone else, Van Alen was told that he would not be working very directly with the senior Chrysler but would instead be dealing with his sons, as this was the very reason Chrysler entered into the enterprise in the first place. He told one reporter, "I was well aware that a rich man's sons are likely to be cheated of something. How could my boys ever know the wild incentive that burned in me from the time I first watched my father put his hand to the throttle of his engine? I could not give them that, but it was through this thinking that I conceived the idea of putting up a building."

In the meantime, while Van Alen was still working on his plans, Chrysler got his crews busy tearing down the five story building that was still standing there. One reporter observed, "In the neighborhood on the easterly Lexington Avenue front between Forty-second and Forty-third Streets, wreckers are tearing down the old row of structures for the proposed sixty-seven-story Chrysler Building, the tower of which will rise 16 feet above the Woolworth Building." Though he said he wanted his sons to take the lead on the project, Chrysler still controlled the purse strings and was very clear about what he wanted: "I want a taller building of a finer type of construction and it's your job to give the best that's in you. ... Improve upon [all other buildings] to the best of your ability. Spare no effort or time." The only thing that Chrysler did not mention, and Van Alen forgot to ask about, was his salary, an omission that would later haunt both of them.

Perhaps inevitably, not everyone was as enthusiastic about the project as the builders were. On February 14, 1929, journalist Charles Driscoll pointed out, "Foes of tall buildings do not make much progress In New York. There are several associations and clubs that work incessantly for laws to prevent the erection of tall buildings in certain districts, and at least one powerful organization that wants the height of buildings restricted all over town. Of course, there are certain restrictions, but for all that, an imaginative and wealthy builder may go as high as he likes into the air. Towers are permitted, with certain technical conditions based upon ground area and other considerations. The Chrysler building, which is already a deep and busy hole in the ground near Grand Central terminal, is to go up 808 feet above the street. That will make it the tallest building in town, topping the Woolworth by 15 or 16 feet." At the same time, as Driscoll noted, those who opposed building bigger skyscrapers didn't stand much of a chance.

As these events were taking place, rumors surfaced that Severance had gone to work for the Bank of Manhattan and was teaming up with the well-known firm of Shreve & Lamb to build his own skyscraper at 40 Wall Street, one predicted to be taller than Chrysler Building. While Van Alen was no doubt unhappy, Chrysler was nearly apoplectic, and he told his architect, "Van, you've just got to get up and do something. It looks as if we're not going to be the highest after all. Think up something. Your valves need grinding. There's a knock in you somewhere. Speed up your carburetor. Go to it!" Severance undoubtedly became an even fiercer competitor when one publication mistakenly assumed Van Alen was the designer of both buildings: "Never, so far as [Van Alen] knew, had an architect been placed in such an awkward position before. Things have been going along in his office strangely—staff divided into two, each side commanded to secrecy, secret codes, two kinds of hog-Latin employed, secret passageways, workmen pledged. All most complicated. What will happen to Mr. Van Alen nobody knows, but observers think it likely that when both buildings are done Mr. Chrysler will probably release a ten-thousand-ton, collapsible, unfolding, one-man top on his building and be countered by No. 1 Wall Street with a semi-floating Zeppelin superstructure, and that the duel will then begin all over again."

40 Wall Street

Chapter 2: Van Alen's Most Radical Design

"Van Alen's most radical design, however, was his original plan for the Reynolds skyscraper, which featured a jewel-like glass dome and a base in which triple-height showroom windows were topped by a full dozen stories with glass-wrapped corners, creating an impression that the massive tower above rested on air...Reynolds evidently disapproved of this advanced and costly scheme. The official 'Reynolds Building' design, published in August, 1928, was a far more conservative venture, with an Italianate dome that one critic said looked like Governor Al Smith's derby hat, and with a brickwork pattern on the upper stories which cleverly (and cheaply) mimicked corner windows, and which is a recognizable feature of the Chrysler Building today. In fact, this design displays the central forms of the existing building exactly: tower, flanks, setbacks, window runs. Yet it differs in everything that makes us think of the Chrysler as unique: the glittering fantasy that defied the austere new modernist ethos (Lewis Mumford awarded the building a 'Booby Prize' for 1930) by turning decorative detail into architectural essence. The transformation began that October, when Reynolds defaulted on his lease and Walter Chrysler was ready with the money, reportedly two million dollars, which got .him the property, the design, and the architect, too." – Claudia Roth Pierpoint, "The Silver Spire" (*New Yorker* November 18, 2002)

On March 4, 1929, after several more months of work, the time finally came for Van Alen to present his plans to Chrysler himself. Historian Neal Bascomb described the scene: "In the automobile man, Van Alen had indeed found the client of a lifetime. Chrysler pushed him, much as he did his car designers. Chrysler requested hundreds of revisions to the architect's first designs. He knew what he liked when he saw it and would pay whatever it cost, but Van Alen had to come up with the ideas. When the architect presented Chrysler with the lobby design, showing him a plaster model with walls painted Morocco-marble red, Chrysler said, 'It looks a little cramped, to me.' Chrysler pointed to one of four columns in the toy-sized lobby. 'A terrific load is carried by those columns in the plans as drawn,' said Van Alen. 'But when people come into a big building, they should sense a change, get a mental lift that will put them in a frame of mind to transact their business—how about this?' He reached his fingers into the toy-sized ground floor lobby and hesitated. 'Pull it out,' said Van Alen. 'That's just a piece of cardboard, pegged in there.' He yanked a cardboard column from the model. 'Could it be done?' Van Alen drew some hurried lines on an envelope with his pencil and then turned it over for him to see. 'It could be done this way.' Chrysler smiled. It was all about impressing the millions of people who would walk through the triangular lobby of his building, costs be damned. Van Alen was with him every step of the way."

Within just a few days of approving them, Chrysler published the blueprints for his new building. According to one reporter, the proposed structure "will be 890 feet in height, making it the highest building in the world, overtopping the 792 feet of the Woolworth Building in lower Broadway. [It will have] elevators: largest vertical transportations; designed so that they can run not only high but as rapidly as 900 feet a minute 'express elevators.'...if run on a non-stop schedule, they would make the entire distance in less than a minute.*"

Another article summarized a bunch of the structure's characteristics:

"-It is estimated by architectures that 11,000 people can be comfortably housed in the building's offices.

-there will be 150 employees to handle traffic

-total are of the plot is 37,555 feet square

-frontage is 167.2 on Forty-second Street; 210.10 on Lexington Avenue and 205 feet in Forty-third Street

-Under the zoning laws of New York City the setback ratio of the building was fixed at one to four.

-There will be 16 stories measuring 182 feet without any setback.

-1st setback is 18 feet in the next 17 stories.

-Properly speaking, the main volume of the story (tower included) is 56 stories. Dome which tops the structure is 12 stories.

-There will be floodlights on each of the four corners of the terrace. (The 56th floor and on the top of the dome; lights the pinnacle of the building.)

-It will be mounted by a sculptures figure six-teen feet high.

-Great hall in street level will sun parallel to Lexington Avenue, north and south.

-Entrance+20 feet wide, 3 stories high (40 feet high)

-The hall will be 100 feet long, 32 feet wide and 26 feet to the cornice, crowned in its center by a dome 38 feet high.

-Special subway entrance will be built in the Forty-second Street and Forty-Third Street corners.

-There will be 2 inside stairways leading to the subways though an arcade which will be lined with shops.

-Face of the building; constructed of imported Norwegian granite AKA 'Shastone' granite.

- Marble; used as high as the fifth floor, from that point to the 16th floor; will be a basketweave pattern of Georgia marble and whitefaces brick.

-Constructors are Fred T. Ley & Co., Inc. The Carnegie Steel Company is
supplying the steel, which will be fabricated by the erected by Post & McCord."

Chrysler likely dreamed of his building being the "jewel in the crown" of New York City, and
Van Alen had a similar vision in mind by designing the Chrysler Building with a positively
jewel-like crown on top. However, when his original design was criticized for resembling New
York Mayor Al Smith's bowler hat, Van Alen soon changed his mind. He later said, "When it
was decided that the topmost part of this building should out-top every other existing structure, it
was necessary to resort to the unusual because of its after-consideration nature. Such problems
are the especial joy of engineers and constructors."

In fact, Van Alen's design was very different than anything that had been conceived of before
since he was obsessed with modernity: "No old stuff for me! No bestial copyings of arches and
colyums and cornishes! Me, I'm new! Avanti!" In speaking of his design for the Chrysler
Building, he explained he was searching for "an architectural character that is effective,
beautiful, and expressive of the purpose of the building, of our method of construction and of the
spirit of the times."

His friend Kenneth Murchison saw him the same way: "Van Alen was the only American
student who returned from Paris without a box full of architectural books. He foresaw the future.
He tingled with the touch of approaching modernism. He threw his pencil compass overboard on
the way home." Another architect, Lewis Sullivan, defined the skyscraper by saying, "It must be
tall, every inch of it tall. The force and power of altitude must be in it, the glory and pride of
exaltation must be in it. It must be every inch a proud and soaring thing."

Chapter 3: A Project for His Sons

"The money came from a personal account. Although Chrysler had been searching for a site
for his business headquarters since he'd set up his corporation, just three years earlier - during
which time it had gone from thirty-second place among car manufacturers to third-this was not a
corporate acquisition. Chrysler wanted the building as a project for his sons, who had suffered
the misfortune of growing up rich, and whom he wished to feel "the wild incentive that burned in
me from the time I first watched my father put his hand to the throttle of his engine." …
Fortune later noted that Chrysler had produced the perfect car for the twenties, "a period when
desires had supplanted needs" - what better definition of being rich? - and it was not long before
he determined to produce the perfect building." – Claudia Roth Pierpoint, "The Silver Spire"
(*New Yorker* November 18, 2002)

Once the plans were completed, they were turned over to Fred T. Ley & Co., the head
contractor for the project. W. A. Starrett, himself no stranger to working on skyscrapers,
explained this process in 1928, "Contractors until now usually had been boss carpenters or
masons, men of a little capital and foremanship, but generally of no technical education, who

executed sub-contracts under the supervision of the architects. This was feasible in small enterprises, but as buildings grew in magnitude architects were overwhelmed with a multiplicity of burdens for which many of them had little training and no aptitude. [George] Fuller raised contracting from a limited trade to both an industry and a profession, visualizing the building problem in its entirety promotion, finance, engineering, labor and materials; and the architect reverted to his original function of design."

By this time, Ley already had his eye on a number of factories that could produce the steel for the soon-to-be famous structure. What was interesting was that it was not the steel traditionally developed for structures that the builders of skyscrapers wanted but that made for bridges. Starrett continued, "While all this activity of foundation building at the site is going on, a hundred things are happening in the office of the skyscraper builder. The structural steel has been ordered, and shop drawings by the ream are being approved and blue- prints of them forwarded to the bridge shop, where men translate them into completed structural members. The bridge shop has furnished the rolling mill with lists of plain shapes and sizes cut to accurate lengths, and it is the business of the bridge shop to take these plain pieces, punch them, rivet on the lugs, build up the columns and girders; all exactly in accordance with the shop drawings. As the pieces are finished, they are marked and numbered in accordance with the setting plans, prepared by the structural engineer as the common guide for all concerned in the design and erection of the steel. For the structural steel is the pivot around which the whole superstructure of the skyscraper under construction turns. Excavation and foundation are timed to the delivery date of the steel, and all plans for enclosing the building must depend on the steel erection."

Even the inside trims were a source of pride, as one small town paper proudly reported in August 1929: "The Metal Door and Trim Co., whose products bear the name 'LaPorte' give this city nation-wide publicity, has been signally honored in receiving the contract for furnishing the swing doors in the unique as well as the tallest building in the world—the Walter P. Chrysler building in New York city. While the local company manufactures metal doors for the largest skyscrapers in the United States, the use of its materials in the Chrysler building further attests to the quality of its doors and trim. The metal door company has already shipped frames for the second to the 56th floor of the Chrysler structure. The skyscraper will stand upon a site owned by the Cooper Union for the Advancement of Science and Art. It will be the tallest inhabitable structure in the world, only exceeded in height by the great French steel skeleton, the Eiffel Tower in Paris."

Next, Ley had to put together a crew to build the mighty structure. Over the life of the project, he would employ the following:

"400 masons and common laborers

130 electrical workers

150 steelworkers

6 riggers

4 roofers

14 waterproof workers

10 asbestos insulators

60 tile layers

25 iron workers

35 workers on sidewalk bridges

8 glaziers

256 plumbers

100 carpenters

100 ventilation workers

20 workers on door bucks

4 marble/stone cutters

3 stone cutters

40 hoisting workers

35 window workers 15 sprinkler system installers

6 steel expediters

4 mail chute installers"

According to Bascomb, there were also "hundreds of other workers, from structural engineers to bricklayers, blacksmiths, master plumbers, concrete workers, derrickmen, sawyers, plasterers, and watchmen. In the end, Chrysler paid for the labor of 2,400 men, 21,000 tons of structural steel, 3,826,000 bricks, 391,881 heated rivets, 794,000 partition blocks, 446,000 tiles, 3,750 plate glass windows, 200 sets of stairs, aluminum railings running two-fifths of a mile, 15 miles of brass strip, 35 miles of pipe, and 750 miles of electric conductor wire. The heaviest columns carried loads of up to seven million pounds."

Of these men, historian Bascomb later wrote, "Safe from the spotlight, the men who actually built these skyscrapers with their sweat and labor worked backstage to the architects and owners eager to settle old scores. They were not dissimilar to the Florentine uomini senza nome e famiglia ('men without name or family') who built Filippo Brunelleschi's dome at the cathedral Santa Maria del Fiore. They worked long days, reported to a foreman who timed their labor by the hour, climbed hundreds of feet by ladder, ate their meals high above the ground, and if hurt on the site, were often left destitute. In their job a careless slip meant a gruesome death, and there were many such accidents. Under the guidance of Rogers, the Chrysler Building site protected the workers better than Brunelleschi could have hoped for his own men, yet for all the watchmen, temporary railings, elevator shaft barricades, tubular scaffolding, and around-the-clock medical aid, only skill and luck prevented a strong gale of wind from unbalancing a riveter and pitching him headlong from the sixty-fourth story. The reward for their work, tallest building or not, arrived on payday."

It was vital that everyone work well together to make the project go smoothly, and every worker was aware that if they didn't pull their weight, they could easily be replaced by someone else. At the same time, there were rewards for those who did their jobs well. Starrett noted, "Interior partitions are of masonry and laid by bricklayers. The superintendent is apt to have directed that the best men from the outside walls be kept and thrown in on partition work. Frequently inclement weather forces a slowing down of the exterior walls, and the competent superintendent has seen to it that some of the floors are stocked with partition tile against this rainy day. The builder knows this also, and has been pushing the architect for any special layouts to be built in floors where the exterior walls are finished. But further description here becomes too complex. The interior requires that interlocking action of steam-fitters, plumbers, electricians, sheet metal workers, elevator constructors and ornamental iron workers, to say nothing of as many more essential trades, with the progress demanding that no nook or corner of the job be idle while work is there to be done."

Workers on one of the Chrysler Building's gargoyles

One of the men working on the Chrysler building was Paul Rockhold, known as the "Prince of Wales of the Girders." Then 30 years old, he already had 15 years of experience working in steel, and he was as tough as it. One time, he decided to ride to the ground on a hoist, and when the hoist slipped and Rockhold plummeted down, he was saved only when the hoist stopped suddenly. According to one report, "The shock of the stop was nearly as bad as the crash would have been. 'Anyone hurt?' a reporter asked him. 'We got our hair rumpled a little. Nerves too perhaps,' Rockhold said. 'Ever been really scared up at the top?' 'Yes, and scared plenty. But when that happens you've got to beat the scare.' 'How?' 'Get fighting mad.'" Rockhold later recalled of his time working steel, "You got to love it and can't quit it. Life down on the street's too slow. Who wants to be a pencil pusher after he's worked with steel…It's nice to point to a mighty 314, nice to point to a mighty suspension bridge or a towering building and say, 'I helped erect that.'"

All those working on the building were organized and skilled. Frank Richards, one of the project's supervisors, once said, "Running up a building's like playing baseball. You've got to have a team. There isn't any more place in a steel gang for the individual star than there is on a baseball team. I pick my own men, and I pick 'em to work together. Sure, to the fellow who never put up a thirty-story building it looks like a simple matter of putting one steel beam against another and riveting 'em together. That's all it is. But you can't rivet a cross-beam unless your two end supports are up to the same height at the same time. That's where the organization and the teamwork comes in. My men know their business."

William Bridges wrote in the *New York Sun*, "When a steel man gets through with a skyscraper it isn't a part of him. It's a good job, or a tough job, or maybe he almost got bumped off while he was working on it, so he remembers it for that reason. As a thing that artists paint and writers strive mightily to describe, he doesn't see a skyscraper. His part of it doesn't show, anyway. The brick masons come along at his heels and cover up the skeleton as fast as he runs it up. It isn't his building when he gets through."

The Chrysler Building under construction in 1930

Chapter 4: A Psychological Phenomenon

"A skyscraper is a psychological phenomenon. Economics have always supplied a justification, but in truth the added costs of building very high - deeper foundations, elevators taking up floor space - were often un-recoupable. In 1929, the American Institute of Steel Construction released a study that reported diminishing returns above the sixty-third floor in midtown Manhattan; nevertheless, it was only the Crash that killed a host of plans for edging up toward where profit was near to nil. The Chrysler dome begins at the building's sixty-sixth floor and officially rises to the seventy seventh, but all the spaces above seventy one are so cramped and contorted that these 'floors' have not been rentable for anything but radio equipment; from the seventy-fifth level up, the jack-o'-lantern windows' are open to the winds. Skyscrapers are about power and longing for transcendence and, as everyone will tell you, about sex: the Empire State Building was known for a time as Al Smith's Last Erection. But the great creators themselves were concerned with an even more profoundly American drive: advertising. And with seeing that the other guy didn't get there first - particularly if the other guy was somebody you knew." – Claudia Roth Pierpoint, "The Silver Spire" (*New Yorker* November 18, 2002)

By early September 1929, the public had become enthralled by all the building going on around Manhattan, but especially the work on the Chrysler Building since it was the farthest along. At the same time, people were also concerned about the long term impact that such tall structures would have on those living and working in them. For example, the *Kingston Daily Freeman* reported, "No doubt New York will take a lot of pride in this building and other cities will narrowly escape civic apoplexy trying to outdo her. Except for the engineering marvel of such structures and when they are well designed, their lovely towers and graceful ascending lines, it is hard to tell what these giant skyscrapers are for. True, they house a great many people and offices. Yet at the same time they play havoc with traffic in the streets below. They shut off sunlight from sidewalks and thoroughfares. They narrow the horizon. They crowd human beings together when elbow room and freedom from the press of crowds are so greatly needed."

The *Freeman* also mentioned another development on the skyscraper front, and one that would cause Chrysler untold grief: "Announcement has just been-made of the building which is to rise on the site of the famous old Waldorf Astoria Hotel at 34th street and Fifth Avenue in New York. The Empire State Building, as this new structure is named, will be nearly 1,000 feet high, towering nearly 200 feet above any existing building in that city of high towers, its 80 stories will carry it 13 floors above the mighty Chrysler building now under construction. The cost will be upwards of $160,000,000, but the cost seems of less importance than the incredible height."

For John J. Raskob, who was the driving force behind the Empire State Building along with former New York Mayor Al Smith, the project was personal. While Raskob had a strong background in business, he knew nothing about real estate; the only thing that mattered to him was that he wanted to build the tallest building in the world. Moreover, he wanted it to be significantly taller than that being built for Chrysler because he had been a chief executive with the company until they pressured him to resign once he got involved in Smith's run for the presidency. While Smith was most interested in the building's location, Raskob was focused on its height, determined to build something taller than the already notorious Chrysler Building.

Raskob

Al Smith

At this point, the Chrysler Building was designed to be 77 stories tall, but it was about to experience a sudden growth spurt. According to architect Kenneth M. Murchison, when Walter Chrysler heard about the Raskob's new project, he ordered his architect to add to the height of his own building. Murchison explained that Van Alen "examined his plans. Right in the center of the tower he found a fire tower which, to the untutored mind, is nothing more or less than a large hole in a building. And there he went secretly to work. He… and [his engineer] evolved a modernistic flagpole of latticed steel.... They named the thing a 'vertix,' because the name hadn't been used before, and they had it made in three pieces. They hoisted it up in the fire tower and there riveted it together."

Not to be outdone, Raskob went back to his architects and demanded that they come up with a taller building. As one man later recalled, "It was a coincidence, [everyone consulted] arrived at a limit of 80 stories." While another five "penthouse" levels could be added, that was it. Of course, there was also the observation deck on the roof, which could be considered a 86th floor, but even without that, Raskob predicted that his building would still be several feet taller than Chrysler's. Still, barely beating out the Chrysler Building was not enough in his eyes, and Hamilton Weber, the Empire State Building's first rental manager, was also concerned: "We thought we would be the tallest at 80 stories. Then the Chrysler went higher, so we lifted the Empire State to 85 stories, but only four feet taller than the Chrysler. Raskob was worried that Walter Chrysler would pull a trick - like hiding a rod in the spire and then sticking it up at the last minute."

By September 4, 1929, construction at the Chrysler Building site was running smoothly and surprisingly on schedule. The steel skeleton of the building was more than 60 stories high and the bricklayers had completed the outside of most of the stories below. There were large derricks operating on both the 26th and 59th floors, each kept busy constantly hauling up new girders and cross pieces to be put in place. Elsewhere, others worked to complete the carefully cut pieces of thick stainless steel that would be pieced together to create the dome.

All the while, the real treasure remained hidden as men worked in the empty fire tower at the top of the building on the "vertex", the secret spire that Van Alen had designed to top the building and win the race to the top. So secret was this portion of the effort that not even the men working on it knew what they were creating, but once completed, it would weigh 27 tons and rise like a spear out of the center of the completed building. In discussing it, Van Alen said, "The tower should grow out of the lower masses surrounding it, and it should terminate in a crowning feature that is a natural and logical development of the tower itself, not merely an ornament placed on the top of the tower. All parts of the design should be tied together in a closely knit composition, each part not only belonging to the whole but accentuating the effectiveness of the other parts."

The adaptation of Van Alen's design for the building

By the fall of 1929, the Chrysler Building was center of public attention, and on October 17, the *New Yorker* proclaimed that Van Alen's "great tower…improves steadily as it progresses. The outlines of the soaring parabolic-dome treatment which will crown its peak are distinctly interesting, as is the modern use of contrasting dark and light material throughout, and the employment of metal panels at various floor levels." Likewise, Francis Swales praised the design, which he said seemed "better than nearly anything I have seen in the design of office buildings during the past several years."

The plans called for the tower to be built in several sections, each set back a few feet on the north and south sides from the one below it, while the east and west sides rose in smooth, unbroken lines. Thus, the first 17 floors, covered with pale Georgian marble and white brick, gave a sense of eternal stability and "an absence of motion," according to Van Alen. Then, near the height of the 24th floor, the structure took on something of a sense of winged movement. The tall windows were flanked by aluminum trim and gave way to more solid floors covered with white brick at the third and fourth level setbacks. Radiator cap shaped gargoyles with 15 feet wingspans adorned the 31st floor, while black and white mosaics graced the floors above and below. Worked in among these Chrysler symbols were inverted Vs from the Van Alen family crest. From this point upward, everything was all about the upward movement; from the shining windows to the black brick, everything was focused on drawing the eye toward the top.

The building under construction

A gargoyle on the Chrysler Building

Chapter 5: Like a Butterfly From Its Cocoon

"On a mild October day in 1929, the architect William Van Alen stood at the corner of Fifth Avenue and Forty-Second Street, shaking with fear as he stared at a spot a few blocks east and very high up. Nearly eighty stories in the air, from out of a dense web of steel, the tip of a needle gleamed and began to climb; Van Alen later wrote that the spire of the Chrysler Building had emerged that day "like a butterfly from its cocoon." But the butterfly stood a hundred and eighty - five feet tall and weighed twenty-seven tons, and nothing like the operation of securing such an object at such an altitude had ever been attempted before. Van Alen reported that he went on shaking whenever he thought about the possible danger to people on the street, who had received no warning of the architectural coup taking place above their heads. … Although the newspapers had been following the skyward contest almost foot by foot, there were no reporters or photographers on hand to share Van Alen's anxious vigil. The spire, a triumph of nerve as much as of ingenuity and steel, was meant to take the city by surprise. The highest thing on the Manhattan skyline rose into view in ninety minutes flat." – Claudia Roth Pierpoint, "The Silver Spire" (*New Yorker* November 18, 2002)

Writing about the progress of the Chrysler Building in his 1929 book *The Metropolis of Tomorrow*, Hugh Ferriss noted, "The excavation across the street proved to be the beginning of the Chrysler building which was to overtop the Chanin — rising, in fact to considerably over eight hundred feet. …the tower looms up freely against the low buildings of the East Side, the river and the horizontal stretches of Long Island. Were we to view it from the opposite direction, it would, however, merge into the great mass of Grand Central skyscrapers (although its unusual terminal curve would still surmount the whole composition) and one might have some foreboding of its effect upon the congestion of Forty-Second and Lexington. It required a considerably more detailed drawing than the one at hand to delineate the many novel effects which, in this design, the architect has ingeniously produced in the fenestration, the brick work and other details which are quite apparent in the building itself; the intention in this sketch is simply to convey an impression of the extreme dimensions which are involved. This extreme tower, however, was scarcely under way before another great excavation was begun a little farther downtown."

The final touch, the "crowning achievement," was the vertex that would make the Chrysler Building taller than all the others. Of course, getting it up to the top was no easy feat, as Van Alen explained: "It was manifestly impossible to assemble this structure and hoist it as a unit from the ground, and equally impossible to hoist it in sections and place them as such in their final positions." But for the moment, it had to remain hidden. As Van Alden put it, "We'll lift the thing up and we won't tell 'em anything about it. And when it's up we'll just be higher, that's all." The "them" he was not going to tell were his competitors working on the Manhattan Bank Building at 40 Wall Street and the Empire State Building, and the cunning plan would succeed in making the Chrysler Building taller than the former before being ultimately topped by the latter.

Most of the people watching the competition for tallest building found it fascinating, or at least amusing, but there were a few that were not so sanguine. Reporter Gilbert Swann wrote in October 1929, "The title of the 'world's tallest building' has become as fragile and transient as a tennis record, a golf championship or a pugilistic leadership. Hardly has a new record been established before a 'bigger and better' building is announced. The Woolworth, far-famed as a tourist attraction, fast threatens to join he pigmies. Within the past couple of weeks, I have watched this race for the skies grow into an elimination contest. I had just become accustomed to watching the Chrysler Building sparing to a height of 808 feet, which is 18 feet beyond the record of the Woolworth, when along came the City Bank and Farmers Trust, which is to build on the old site of the Waldorf-Astoria, would climb to 925 feet, making all others look meager and stunted in growth. … Consideration of such gargantuan competition causes even hard-boiled New Yorker to breathe rapidly. … But what causes the shivers to start creeping is not so much the height of the forecasted building, but the inevitable problems in congestion they will create. I have no way of knowing how many people will occupy a 1,050- foot building, or a 925-foot building. Much smaller skyscrapers boast that three or four thousand people pass through their doors daily. How will the people who occupy these new places find transit to and from their homes? Again, the narrow streets have never been widened to accommodate the growth of traffic which must, inevitably, follow. With congestion already at its peak, how can the materials be handled without further complicating matters? Sooner or later Manhattan is going to have to face a few such problems—and even I may yet wind up on a Connecticut farm before it's through."

On November 10, Severance thought he had won the race for tallest building when he placed his marble capstone on the top of the Manhattan Bank Building, but he soon learned he was wrong. In a story published a few days later in the *Daily Building Report*, a reporter let the secret of the vertex out: "This is the story of how two architects, formerly partners, vied with each other to erect two of the world's tallest man-made habitable structures, and how one of them, by an ingenious engineering device, finally succeeded in passing the hitherto thousand-foot pinnacle of the Eiffel Tower in Paris . . . While the structural steel men were fabricating in the shops the final-framework for the lantern story on the Bank of Manhattan Building . . . there was being secretly fabricated 845 feet above 42nd Street at Lexington Avenue a spindle-like lattice ornament that only a few knew what it was to be used for . . . It grew in size two, three, four, until finally it reached a dozen stories tall before it dawned upon the workmen on the job that it was some kind of a pinnacle, but how was it going to be set, on so narrow and so precarious a footing as the structural steel beams and columns and girders more than 845 feet above the street, until the day came when a huge American flag, attached to its point, floated out 100 feet beyond the derrick boom that raised it, and the 185 foot vertex was fitted into place as the Stars and Stripes straighten out at the highest level the Flag ever flew from a fixed point in New York City—the top of the world's highest man-made structure."

A few weeks later, Chrysler and Van Alen took a makeshift elevator and then a series of precarious ladders to stand atop what was at that moment the tallest building in the world. In trying to describe what they must have felt, author David Michaelis mused, "Deep-sea divers in deep-sea depth are said to experience something called the rapture of the deep. A diver's euphoria proves so overwhelming that he fails to return to the surface even when his air runs outs. From the 84th floor of the Chrysler Building, the city below appears as dreamy, distant, and unnecessary as the mercury-colored surface of the sea must look to an enraptured diver."

It is hard for anyone else to conceive of how Van Alen felt that glorious day. In fact, he later claimed that it was not the building's height that made his heart swell but the "natural and logical development of the tower. ... With all the surfaces of this spire turned toward the sky, it will reflect nothing but the sky, and because it will have no outline—all being in perfect reflection—it is expected to be almost invisible. Thus the tower will appear to join the sky and melt into any cloud that floats by." When all the work was done, the magnificent spire would be flanked by eight eagles made of the same polish stainless steel, not the "rusticated stone work, belt courses and heavy stone cornices," that he despised. The eagle shaped gargoyles would feature a "very bold in outline, form and scale, and of proportions suitable for their great altitude."

The Chrysler Building in 1931

Chapter 6: Dome and Spire

Picture of the ornamentation near the top

Picture of the Chrysler Building from the ground

"The Chrysler dome and spire…were clad in a revolutionary metal that looked like an alloy of steel and light. The use of diamond-honed Enduro KA-2 steel, developed by Krupp in Germany after the First World War and exhibited for the first time in 1926, was Chrysler's most significant decision. He had had it tested for months, to be sure that no amount of exposure would tarnish its almost metaphysical silver glow. When the top of the building was revealed, in 1930, critics marveled at the incandescence that made it a beacon even to ships far out at sea; not a single metal sheet has ever been replaced, and on clear days the Chrysler tower is still outshone only by the sun itself. But the first extensive architectural use of stainless chromium-nickel steel provided more than a gleaming surface for Van Alen's design; it appears to have provided an inspiration. Conjecture about the source and meaning of the Chrysler's majestically heaped-up arches and triangles has ranged from car wheels (with spokes) to a chorus girl's headdress (with feathers) to Angkor Wat. In Van Alen's mind, the origins seem related to the imaginative leap from glass and brick to the possibilities of steel.... But the giant star may still be seen, visibly transformed into architecture, in the silver dome's radiating burst of jagged, sharp cornered windows." – Claudia Roth Pierpoint, "The Silver Spire" (*New Yorker* November 18, 2002)

As the building came to completion, Chrysler ordered a brochure on his building published, and it contained the following poetic summary of much of what he felt about it: "Heavenward spring the spires of man's aspiration. Through the ages, from the eternal pyramids brooding over Egypt's timeless sands, the soul has sought expression in a restless, ceaseless striving to reach the heights . . . And now, one more bold has attained a new eminence . . . into the glorious sky of eternal blue and billowy cloud springs the shining finial, fashioned of gleaming metal and flaunting its triumph like the upraised lance of a knight of old."

An Indiana newspaper reported on December 10, 1929, "Walter P. Chrysler announces that the Chrysler building, with steel construction completed, rises to a total height of 1,030 feet. The structure now is the tallest which ever has been erected anywhere in the world, according to Mr. Chrysler, who is president of the W. P. Chrysler Building corporation. Supremacy in high construction which has remained with the city of Paris for the last forty years, since the Eiffel Tower was completed in 1889, is now transferred to New York. The Chrysler building exceeds by more than 100 feet the height of the second tallest habitual structure in the world. Rising skyward more than 1,000 feet, the building in its uppermost part is well above the 9114-foot Eiffel tower, the 925-foot Manhattan Company building and the 792- foot Woolworth building."

Perhaps no one enjoyed the sight of progress as much as Chrysler himself, for while he claimed that his sons were in charge of the building, he was the one who really loved the project. In January 1930, he told a reporter, "I got a thrill watching this building go up, floor after floor. It was inspiring. I've stood on the sidewalk across the street day after day watching this building go up and to say it thrilled me is putting it lightly. It is a credit to craftsmanship." The article went on, "It is seventy-eight stories high, dwarfing the fifty-six story Woolworth building, and is even higher than the Eiffel Tower in Paris. It represents a $16,000,000 investment on Mr. Chrysler's part and is located in the heart of New York, near the Grand Central Station. ... The towering structure which pierces the clouds high up over the busiest metropolis in the world stands as a silent tribute to this man who rose to his present eminent position from an errand boy in a grocery store at Ellis, Kansas. Chrysler was not so proud on his own account as he was over what the mammoth structure represents. He had in his visionary way believed it was inevitable that New York would have a building that would stand as a symbol of what has been achieved in American industry, and that is what he believes the Chrysler skyscraper. ... He personally congratulated the laborers who built it, as 'worker to worker.'"

On Valentine's Day 1930, as the nation reeled under the burden of an ever-worsening economic depression, an optimistic interview with Van Alen appeared in a New York newspaper: "'Seventy-eighth floor, please.' This will soon be a common, every day salutation to elevator operators at the new Chrysler Building, seventy-eight stories high, the tallest structure in the world which is almost ready for occupancy. The first tenant probably will be the Texas-Company which is scheduled to move in April 1. The beautiful new Chrysler Building, its tower piercing the clouds, dwarfs the other tall structures in New York City. It is slightly over 1,000 feet high,…even taller than the Eiffel tower in Paris. With a tinge of pride in his voice, William Van Alen, prominent New York architect, who conceived the new $15,000,000 Chrysler building, referred to it as -- 'the most modern building in America.' - 'It is my interpretation of what a real skyscraper should be.' Mr. Van Alen told International News Service. 'It is an entirely different type of architecture and based on my studies of buildings in America and Europe. Instead of the usual vertical lines this building is a combination of vertical and horizontal lines, the horizontal lines being used to accentuate the vertical lines. One of the new things about the building is its metal coping and metal ornamentation.' Asked if he believed that even higher buildings than this one would be built, the architect replied affirmatively. The height limit of a structure with the steel and materials available at present is between 2,000 and 7,500 feet, he said. He added that the height of a building 'is determined by the size of its plot and by its elevators.' The elevators in the new Chrysler building will number thirty-four and will be self-operating—the button type. 'Skyscrapers help make a city beautiful in appearance,' said Van Alen. 'What is more beautiful than New York's skyline with its inspiring skyscrapers in the forefront? I believe the new Chrysler building will have its effect on other future skyscrapers all over the country. The tendency in big cities is increasing toward the skyscraper because of its economic advantages.' There are now 377 skyscrapers in the United States, half of which are located in New York City were the new Chrysler building assumes a dominant position."

Determined to win back his fans from the newly announced Empire State Building, the builder in mid-December hired famed female photographer Margaret Bourke-White "to steeple jack for Mr. Chrysler." Though only 23 years old, she had worked for Chrysler before and shared his love for modern industry, once writing, "Industry is huge and vital. It is important because it is close to the heart of the people. Art must be sincere and active to have value. Art that springs from industry should have real flesh and blood, because industry itself is the vital force of this great age."

Bourke-White

Referring to her experience working for Chrysler and Van Alen during this period, she later wrote, "In this battle of the skyscrapers, the chief contenders were the ply-foot Bank of Manhattan and the unfinished Chrysler Building, slated to rise to more than 1,000 feet, and I was brought in as a sort of war correspondent on the Chrysler side. The scene of battle was that relatively narrow band of atmosphere ranging from 800-1,200 feet above the sidewalks of New York…a principal target was prestige. A skyscraper was a tall and strong feather in the cap of that ultra-rare individual who could afford to build one. … Certainly Mr. Walter Percy Chrysler was aware of the stupendous advertising value generated when the world's highest building bears the name of your product. And this was where I came in. A dastardly rumor had been circulated, undoubtedly by some busy banker, that the Chrysler Building would not actually surpass the Bank of Manhattan, despite the Chrysler claim of total supremacy at 1,046 feet. The insinuation was that the Chryslers were merely pasting on an ornamental steel tower to gain the few feet needed to make the world's record. I had been photographing the mile-long Chrysler factory in Detroit and was given the job in New York of taking progress pictures of each stage of construction to show that the tower was an integral part of the building. The Chryslers need not have gone to such lengths to prove their supremacy, because in one short year it did not matter anyway. All the man-made structures of this planet would be topped by a spire rising to the magnificent height of 1,250 feet, freezing the world's altitude record to date, and built by a man named Smith."

Chapter 7: The New Metal's Glow

"Also clad in the new metal's glow were the nine-foot-high pineapples and colossal radiator caps and fierce eagle heads that animate the building's corners like grotesques looming out from a medieval cathedral. …a brick frieze depicting hubcaps zipped around the thirtieth floor, punctuated by those imperial radiator caps with wingspans of fifteen feet. …the perfect model eagle glowers just a block away, thrusting its head straight out from behind the wing-capped god Mercury - who looks, under the circumstances, oddly like the radiator-capped god Mercury…. The towering Chrysler eagles evoke the power that trains and steam and shrieking speed once had over the imagination…. There is a boy's sense of scale and wonder in all the building's details and public spaces, whether they look backward to Kansas or forward to a sort of Emerald City, which a population of office workers entered every day through granite portals shaped like Egyptian tombs and flecked with mother-of-pearl. Yet, after passing through the lobby, with its rouge flamme marble walls, and riding up in elevators styled like tiny Parisian drawing rooms, most people found themselves set down amid plain white walls and dull square windows-mere real life. Van Alen did what he could to keep this sad phenomenon at bay, with elaborate radiator grilles and patterned doorknob, but the economic reality of so many floors had to be conceded." – Claudia Roth Pierpoint, "The Silver Spire" (*New Yorker* November 18, 2002)

The vertex was designed to make the Chrysler Building the tallest, but naturally, that didn't stop the arguments over which building was tallest because some people only wanted to count the parts that could actually be used by people, much the same way officials in Chicago recently argued the Sears Tower is taller than New York City's new Freedom Tower. As one of the contractors working on the Empire State Building pointed out, "Chrysler's only sixty-eight stories. We're seventy. They put that flagpole, or whatever they call it, on the top, and it goes up higher, but you can't put offices in a flagpole, can you? We've got more construction. Clear up to the top penthouse, right under the pole, we've got space for things you have to put in a building like this."

Similarly, in March 1930, Yasuo Matsui, who had helped design the Manhattan Bank Building, wrote, "Generally speaking, one thinks of Cleopatra's Needle as an obelisk in Central Park, but William Van Alen's skyline project is truly a sharp steel needle. We have been told that this has been done by a patented method and secret plan . . . The legitimate height of skyscrapers should be considered of the building only, in accordance with the Building Code, and shouldn't include the flagpole or the radio needle, so the Eiffel Tower still holds the crown for the highest structure, its observatory being 905 feet, 11 inches above grade. The Bank of The Manhattan Company's tower on Wall Street ranks second, its observatory being 836 feet, 5 inches above the Wall Street grade. A good third is the Chrysler Building, its observatory being 783 feet, 1 1/2 inches above Lexington avenue grade, or 53 feet below that of the Bank of the Manhattan Building . . . the growth of skyscrapers is only by public demand and economic necessity. Therefore purely ornamental towers, such as the Metropolitan and the Woolworth of today, have no particular significance from a commercial standpoint."

As the Chrysler building neared completion, speculation spread throughout the country about how it would ultimately look and if it was even actually safe. On February 2, 1930, Robert Potter, writing for the *Syracuse Herald*, observed, "Higher and higher go the skyscrapers which make New York the structural wonder of the modern world, and architects hint that, the only obstacles preventing them from scaling the Heavenly heights are lack of somebody else's money to build with, and a sufficiently large available site. Chrysler and Chanin together with Lefcourt and Frenchy and Smith could probably build to within hearing distance of the music of the angels. But the competitive spirit that animates the building fraternity [drives the] experiment. This race to build the highest structure in the world is still a man-to-man affair. Perhaps they figure the reward is greater that way. Likewise it is somewhat of a week-to-week matter, when one credits paper buildings much as one does paper profits in the market. For the moment Alfred K. Smith has outsmarted all competitors with his plan to top the 1,100- foot tower of the 85 story Empire State Building with a 200 foot dirigible mooring mast. Fred French has only just announced his plans to build up 1,100 feet on the site on the old Hippodrome Theater, and he may have learned from Walter P. Chrysler the publicity value of keeping a secret until the shingles are being put on the roof of the tower. For the Chrysler Building at Lexington Avenue and Forty-Second Street, which started out to be a mere 65-story building 600 feet high, has grown…during the course of construction to 1,030 feet, making it the tallest structure in the world, not excepting the Eiffel Tower in Paris. A competition developed between the architects for the Chrysler Building and the Bank of the Manhattan Company Building at 40 Wall Street. Last October the Bank of the Manhattan Company claimed the victory by 23 feet, but in November the Chrysler Building won, when it was suddenly crowned with a lattice work vertex and pinnacle."

Not only was the competition fun to watch, it all drove the builders to literally greater and greater heights. However, with this progress came real concerns on the part of those who would have to live with it. Potter continued, "Without a doubt, this competitive building of biggest and highest buildings is one of the most interesting phases of New York life. Probably no other sport or activity, not even attempting to beat the stock market, has more fervent or rabid fans. There's not a 32-story building constructed in New York but what its progress is watched day and night, from the sinking of foundations to stringing the flagpole, by these curious people. Many seem to devote their lives to it. Their predicament must become quite difficult as the number of buildings under construction increases and some of these building fanciers may have to be retired to the psychopathic ward at Bellevue. Considerably more serious, as a result of the geographical concentration of the new skyscrapers, will be the predicament of the tens of thousands of people who will work in them. Even without their added numbers transit facilities are already taxed to insufferable capacity and Mayor Walker is certainly no magician when it comes to building subways or providing busses. Forty-Second Street is the scene of the …feverish activity in skyscraper construction. The Chanin Building, with a capacity of more than 10,000 tenants, is already completed and occupied. It is just across the way from the Chrysler Building, which will shortly be housing a larger number. … So New York is pouring the populations of fair-sized cities into its new towers, and the towers are rising almost cornice to cornice in midtown end in the financial district. And besides the 10 to 15 thousand population for every one of them. It is estimated that nearly 100,000 persons pass through the doors of such buildings in the course of the day's business hours. The theory of it all is beautiful, the concentration of people means the concentration of business, and that means more work done in less time, more profits per square inch of ground or per minute, and so everybody is very happy—until one tries to get home. Just where the Mayor's city planning commission fits into this delightful scheme of things, it is rather difficult to see."

Ferriss agreed with these concerns and added, "If one thinks of the vast number of people who are housed in a single vertical column during business hours, one must go some to visualize all of them spreading out, over the immediately adjoining streets at 5 in the afternoon. Indeed, it has sometimes been suggested that an architect when designing a structure to house 10,000 souls, should be required to take it as part of his commission to see that facilities have been provided for taking them to and from their 10,000 respective homes. Fortunately, there is already a stirring among architects in the direction of more active participation in civic planning. ... I am most interested in seeing the city develop along as humanitarian lines as possible. There is no chance of bringing about decentralization. But centralization as it is being developed today by real estate promoters means increasing inconvenience and trouble for everyone. I believe that the large skyscrapers of the near future should stand apart from each other with a block or so of intervening low buildings. Only In that way will there be sun and light and air for all."

Chapter 8: A Crown of Stars

"Only at the level of the Cloud Club did fantasy resume. Occupying three linked stories at the base of the dome, this executives' lunch club (which doubled as a speakeasy in its early years) was a stylistic riot of Georgian lobby, Tudor lounge, and Bavarian bar. The main dining room, however, was pure cosmopolitan "Cheek to Cheek": faceted blue marble columns with white-ice sconces that melted into a vaulted ceiling painted with clouds. Not many people got to see these clouds; membership was reserved for the likes of E. F. Hutton and Conde Nast. But for fifty cents anyone could go up to the observatory, on the seventy-first floor, where the steeply tilted walls reflected structural necessity masked as pure design through a close look at Expressionist film sets.... The observatory was open for only a few years, but photographs reveal that its decor of painted sun rays and ringed Saturn lighting globes gave the glorious space an unlikely, naive sweetness - an optimism that seems to emanate from the prominent reliquary like case in which, there at the summit, Walter Chrysler enshrined his first set of machinist's tools. But the room itself enshrined an essential characteristic of the Chrysler and Van Alen enterprise: the determined innocence that turned Krupp steel into a crown of stars, and revamped the geometry of angst into an Art Deco heaven for the workingman." – Claudia Roth Pierpoint, "The Silver Spire" (*New Yorker* November 18, 2002)

Finally, opening day came and the Chrysler Building began its short lived reign as the tallest building in the world. An editorial in the *Olean Times*, written on May 31, 1930 gushed, "A world championship changed hands on Tuesday when Mr. Cass Gilbert's Woolworth Tower bowed, ever so gracefully, to Mr. William Van Alen's Chrysler Building. The latter is now the tallest structure ever designed for regular human occupancy. How long will the Chrysler Building retain this new title won by a mighty effort right at the tape from the onrushing Bank of the Manhattan Company tower? Not for very long, it may be safely predicted. Only let us climb out of temporary business recession and the welkin over Manhattan Island will be ringing to new riveters' choruses. ... The Chrysler Building, with its cupola and flag structure of chromium, its metal gargoyles, its characteristic use of materials and design and color, in interior decoration, shows markedly the "modern" influence. It is modern in the same sense as its close neighbor and predecessor by several years, the American Radiator Building, is modern in exotic black and gold. By comparison the plain white minaret of the Woolworth Tower would be a mid-Victorian spinster."

Topping it all off was the type of place that made women of the generation sigh and women of the next generation scream. According to one account, the Chrysler building featured an "Eveless Eden! Among Clouds of Skyscraper." The article asserted, "The mere male at last has found a retreat where the merry modern woman cannot plant her pretty heels— but he's had to go up sixty-six stories to do it. The Cloud Club, one of the most expensive and exclusive luncheon clubs in the world, has opened its doors on the three top floors of the sixty-eight-story Chrysler Building and no wife, mother or sweetheart is going to put her foot in there. Only one woman is allowed within its portals. She is Miss Josephine Riley, the petite brunette telephone operator whose first and foremost business is to see that the primary rule of the club is obeyed. The membership of the organization includes the names of Vanderbilt, Firestone, Whitney and Chrysler; its view embraces two rivers, a harbor and distant mountain peaks; and its food, furnishings and knick knacks are the most unobtrusively expensive that can be found. Even a cigar costs $2."

Still, the reviews of the new building can best be described as mixed. On one hand, the editor of the *Architectural Forum* said, "It stands by itself, something apart and alone. It is simply the realization, the fulfillment in metal and masonry, of a one-man dream, a dream of such ambition and such magnitude as to defy the comprehension and the criticism of ordinary men or by ordinary standards." On the other hand, George S. Chappell, writing for *The New Yorker*, complained, "The tower of the Chrysler Building, as we have said, stands revealed in all its gleaming glory. It is distinctly a stunt design, evolved to make the man in the street look up. To our mind, however, it has no significance as serious design; and even if it is merely advertising architecture, we regret that Mr. Van Alen did not arrange a more subtle and gracious combination for his Pelion-on-Ossa parabolic curves. The addition of the needle-like spire on top may be dismissed as an over-ambition gesture on the part of the owners of the building. We cannot help feeling, too, that all this exposed sheet metal is a part of temporary construction, to be covered up later with masonry. No doubt we are not yet used to the new methods of using building materials."

In a 1931 article entitled "Notes on Modern Architecture," Lewis Mumford was heavily critical of the skyscraper: "The ornamental treatment of the [Chrysler Building] facade is a series of restless mistakes [which] could easily have been corrected by a plain, factual statement of the materials . . . Such buildings show one the real dangers of a plutocracy; it gives the masters of our civilization an unusual opportunity to exhibit their barbarous egos, with no sense of restraint or shame. Among the many blessings of depression, one must count the diminution of such opportunities."

As fate would have it, the one person who had poured his heart and soul into the building was the one who would enjoy it the least. Van Alen learned shortly after he completed the project that

Chrysler did not plan to pay him for his work; instead, the automobile mogul accused the somewhat naïve architect of taking kickbacks from those hired to work on the project. During the time in which the work was actually going on, Chrysler paid Van Alen a substantial salary of $8,000 a month, and in his eyes, that amount and the $100,000 he had paid Van Alen to buy out the contract he had previously held with Reynolds was more than enough for his work. However, Van Alen countered that he was owed in the neighborhood of $800,000 or six percent of the building's total cost, a standard fee for architects at that time.

Both men remained stubborn, so their lawyers stepped in, with Van Alen ultimately filing suit against Chrysler and getting a lien on the building itself until he was paid. Chrysler knew that if Van Alen won his case in court, he could demand that the building be sold and he be given a share of the profits. Since no one wanted that to happen, a heated battle ensued, leading the *American Architect* to hold up the incident as "a lesson to other architects who are inclined to depend on their artistic rather than on their business ability."

Eventually, both sides took depositions, examined documents and called witnesses, and while Van Alen ultimately won the battle, he lost the war. While he did indeed force Chrysler to pay him for his work, he also gained such a bad reputation with the press that he was never able to find real work in the city again. As one author later noted, "There was not much to do for an architect of gaudy skyscrapers in the 1930's, but Van Alen tried other fields. In 1934 he published a design for a modernistic copper-clad house to be mass produced, and in 1936 he erected a similar steel house as a demonstration on a vacant lot at 39th Street and Park Avenue. The developer Charles Paterno built an apparent twin at the southeast corner of 107th Street and Riverside Drive in the same year. In 1938 Van Alen lost his Lexington Avenue site in foreclosure."

Unbowed, and in what would be his final show of courage and pluck, Van Alen made waves at the Beaux Arts Architectural Ball in January 1931 when he arrived dressed as his own masterpiece, complete with a towering silver and black headdress that made him by far the tallest person in the room.

In 1932, journalist Elmer Davis wrote a final sad statement against the great skyscraper competition that the Chrysler Building had ignited: "So there they stand, those magnificent monuments to the faith of the nineteen twenties—a perpetual inspiration to the beholder, provided he never invested any money in them. What is to become of them? The setback skyscrapers of Babylon have crumbled into hills of mud, but steel and concrete do not melt so easily. Of the faith that built the cathedrals of Ile-de-France, enough has survived to keep those buildings in repair; but the faith that built the Empire State and Chrysler buildings may presently be as dead as Bel and Marduk.

Whether the faith was dead or not is a matter of opinion, but the Chrysler Building was and is still quite alive and bustling, even more today than it was 80 years ago.

The Chrysler Building from the Empire State Building

Bibliography

Bascomb, Neal (2003). *Higher: A Historic Race to the Sky and the Making of a City.* Crown Publishing Group. Kindle Edition.

Stravitz, David (2002). *The Chrysler Building: Creating a New York Icon Day by Day.* New York: Princeton Architectural Press.

Terranova, Antonio; Manferto, Valeria (2003). *Skyscrapers.* Vercelli, Italy: White Star.

Printed in the USA
CPSIA information can be obtained
at www.ICGtesting.com
LVHW011615211223
767129LV00009B/400